One Deep Breath

By

Jennie Mae Harper

Oliver stood nice and proud, with a bright red shirt, and a big wide smile.

He stood in line right next to his mom and held her hand tight.
They waited patiently to get a team as the big yellow sun was shining bright.

Oliver looked up at his mom and said, "Oh how I hope I get a team with lots of friends, with real cool jerseys, and lots of fans."

"You will son," his mom said. "You're the greatest kid!"

But deep inside Oliver was scared to meet people for the first time.
He was shy and did not understand why.

Oliver's mom looked down and exclaimed, "You're going to be the star of the team!"

"Congratulations, you are a Red Sox player!" the big coach yelled.
The big coach smiled and said, "I can't wait to see your skills out on the field."

Oliver looked down to the ground.
His heart was racing, and he began to frown.

He thought to himself, oh no! I must play in front of all these people.
What if they laugh and I make mistakes?
What if I fall right on my face?

Oliver's mom whispered in his ear, "You are the greatest player of the year.
Hold your head up and let them see you shine. One deep breath, one step at a time."

"You're up to bat!" the big coach screamed.
Oliver scurried over to his team.

With shaky arms and sweaty hands, Oliver looked anxiously at all the fans.

"**STRIKE ONE!**" the umpire shouted in Oliver's ear.
Oliver looked over at his mom sitting in her bright blue chair.

His mom smiled and whispered into the air,
"Let them see you shine, one deep breath, one step at a time."

"**STRIKE TWO!**" the umpire shouted in Oliver's ear. Now Oliver was shaking with fear.

Oliver gripped the bat and pulled down his hat, and opened his mouth to say...
"Let the world see me shine. One deep breath, one step at a time."

Oliver blew out a deep breath and looked the pitcher in the eyes.
He watched the ball come toward him one step at a time, and THEN...

The crowd went wild! The team was screaming, and his mother was gleaming, as Oliver hit a **HOMERUN!**

Oliver ran to all the bases and he was proud.
He faced his fears in front of a crowd.

And as he touched every base, he whispered to himself.
"Let the world see you shine. One deep breath, one step at a time."

9 798348 217778